Cross Stitch

Alphabets to Stitch

4 ABC   **5** ABC   **5** ABC

6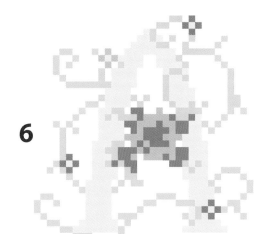

11 Aa Bb Cc   **11** ABC

12 ABC   **13** ABC   **13** ABC

14 ABC   **16** ABC

15 ABC

LEISURE ARTS, INC. • Little Rock, Arkansas

Designed by Jennifer Mitchell

CROSS STITCH

ANCHOR		DMC	COLOR
387	K	Ecru	Ecru
253	F	472	Ultra Light Avocado Green
870	P	3042	Light Antique Violet

If you want to incorporate the background, stitch the desired letter first. Then, using the background chart, stitch the background to complete the design, being sure your letter is centered within the background.

4

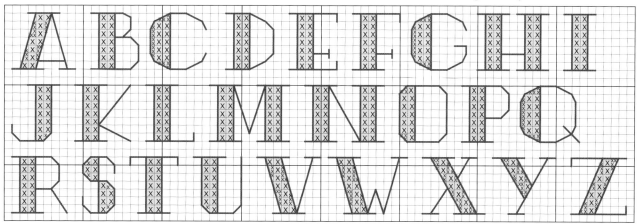

CROSS STITCH				BACKSTITCH		
ANCHOR		DMC	COLOR	ANCHOR	DMC	COLOR
851	X	924	Very Dark Gray Green	851 ———	924	Very Dark Gray Green

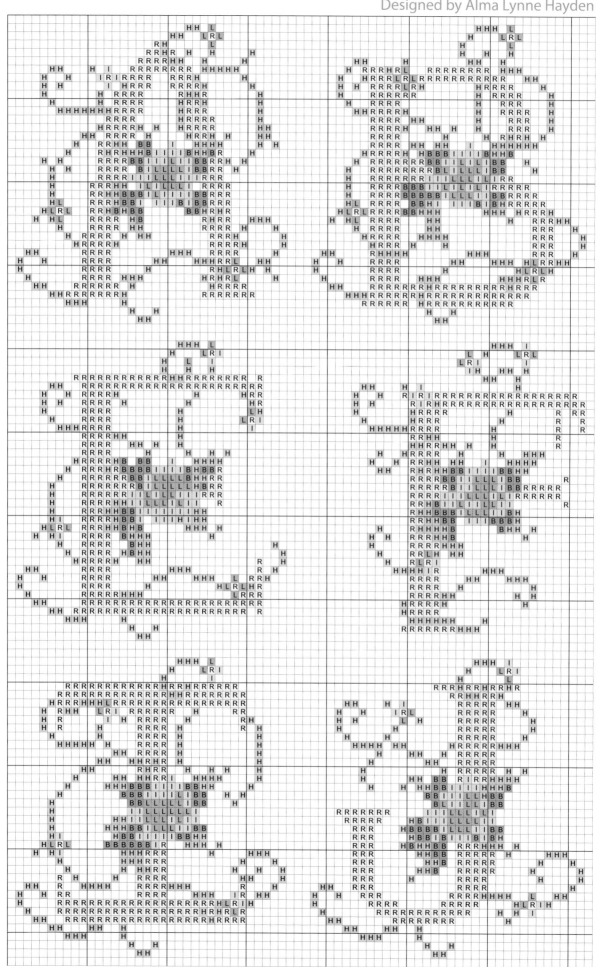

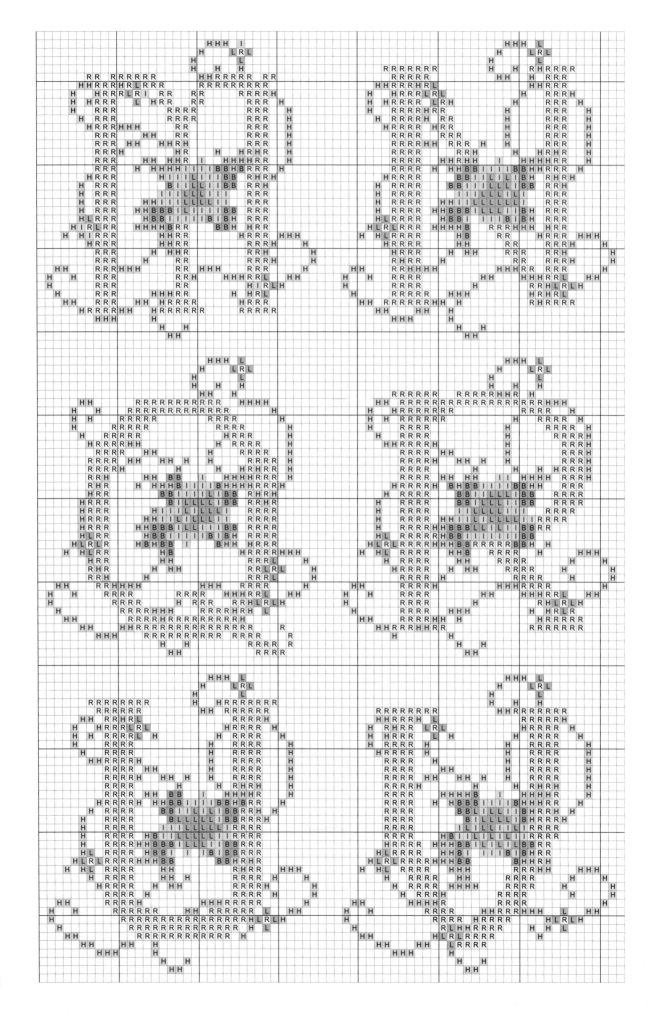

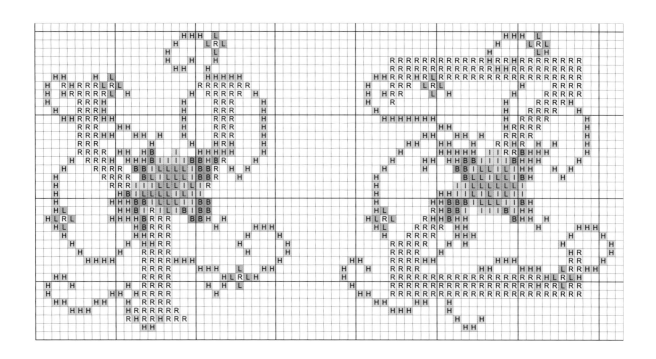

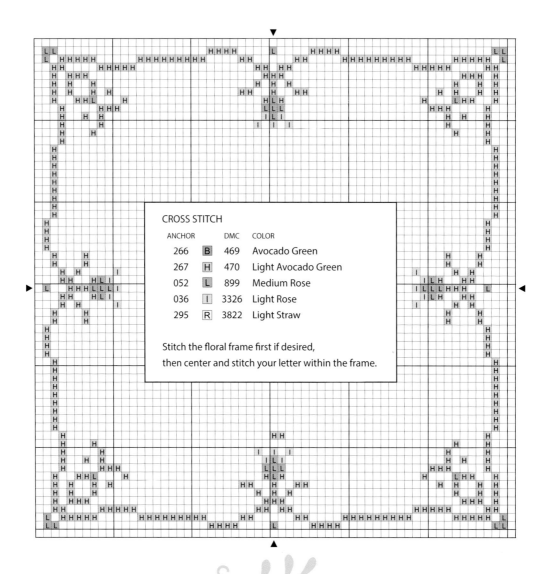

CROSS STITCH

ANCHOR		DMC	COLOR
266	B	469	Avocado Green
267	H	470	Light Avocado Green
052	L	899	Medium Rose
036	I	3326	Light Rose
295	R	3822	Light Straw

Stitch the floral frame first if desired,
then center and stitch your letter within the frame.

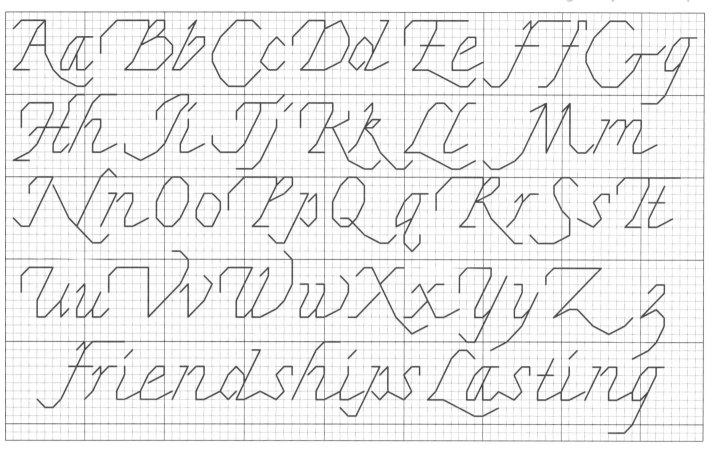

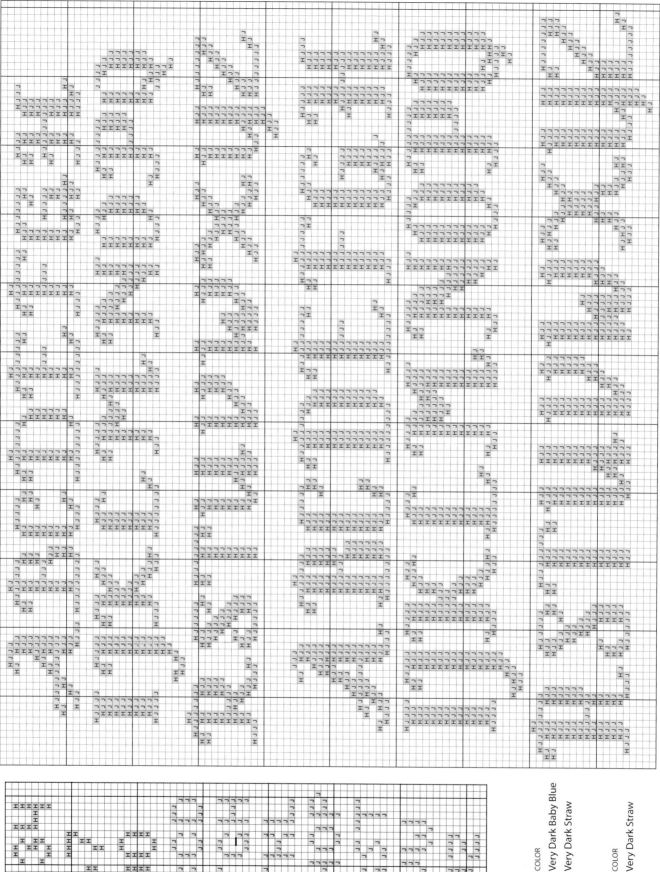

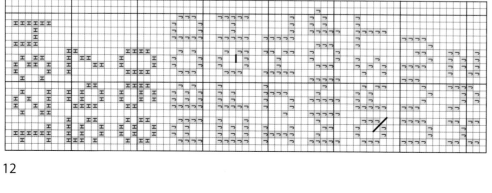

12

CROSS STITCH

ANCHOR		DMC	COLOR
979	H	312	Very Dark Baby Blue
306	J	3852	Very Dark Straw

BACKSTITCH

ANCHOR		DMC	COLOR
306	——	3852	Very Dark Straw

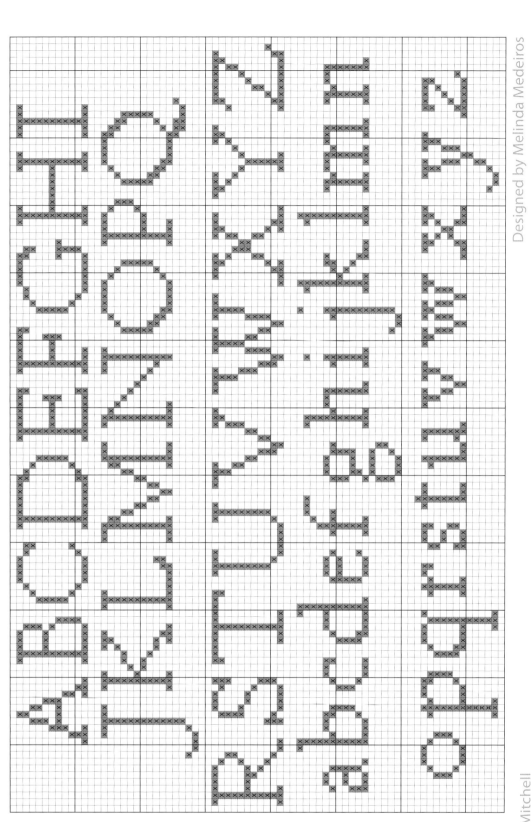

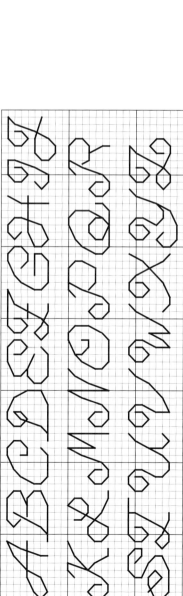

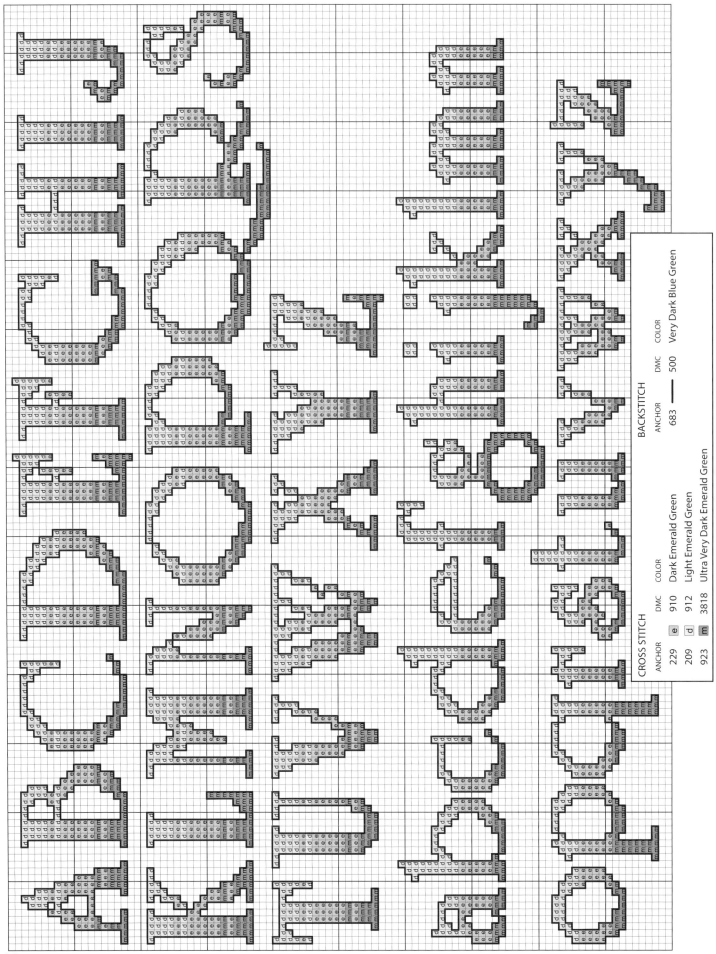

CROSS STITCH

ANCHOR	DMC	COLOR
229	e 910	Dark Emerald Green
209	d 912	Light Emerald Green
923	m 3818	Ultra Very Dark Emerald Green

BACKSTITCH

ANCHOR	DMC	COLOR
683	—— 500	Very Dark Blue Green

CROSS STITCH

ANCHOR		DMC	COLOR
334	T	606	Bright Orange Red
256	U	704	Bright Chartreuse

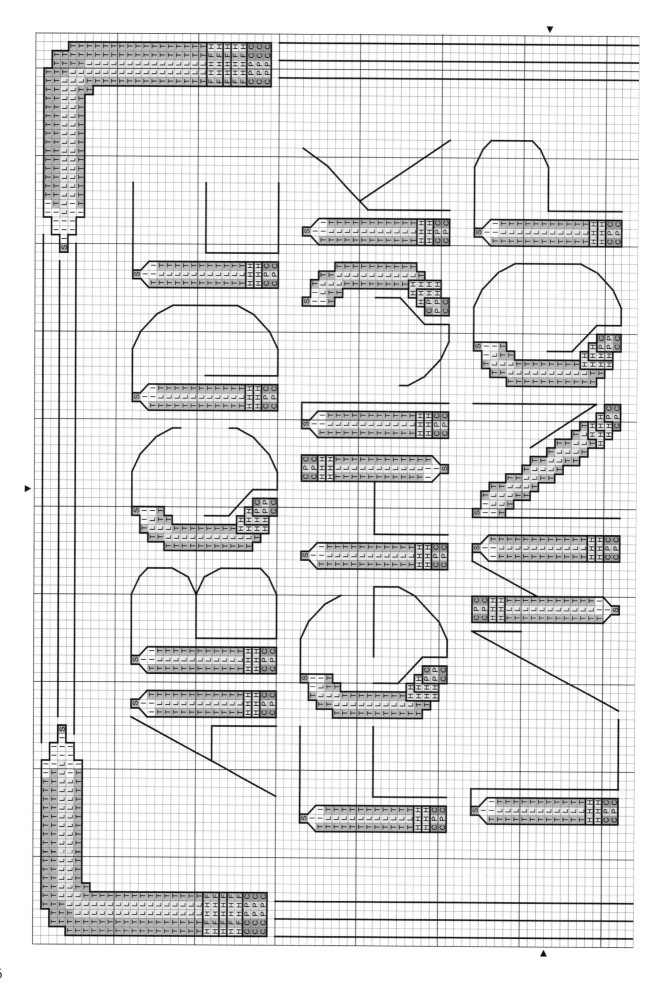

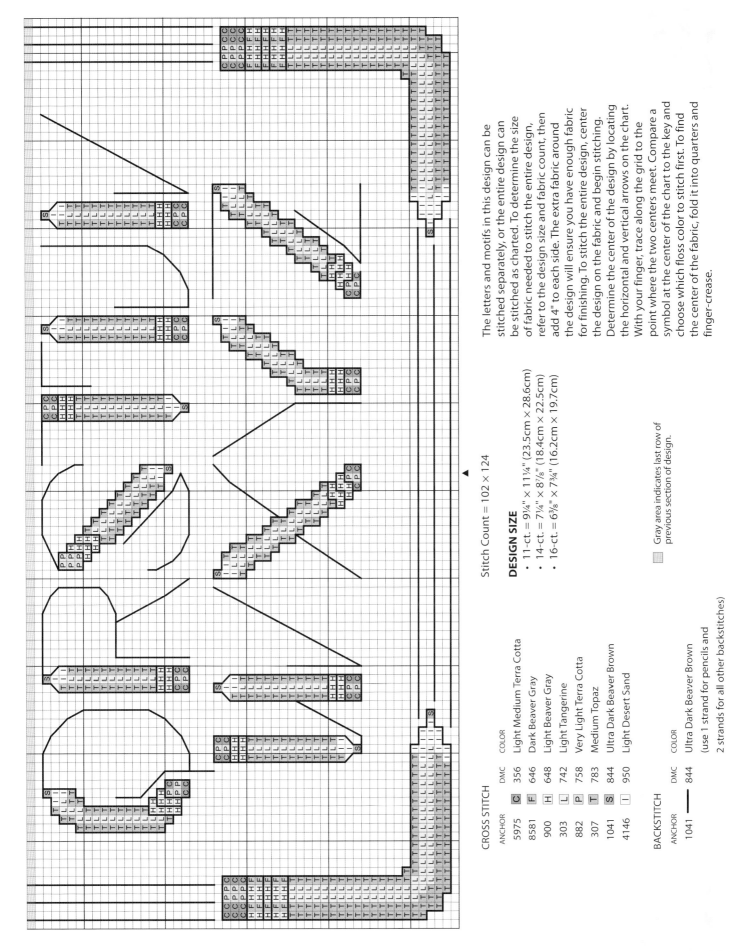

The letters and motifs in this design can be stitched separately, or the entire design can be stitched as charted. To determine the size of fabric needed to stitch the entire design, refer to the design size and fabric count, then add 4" to each side. The extra fabric around the design will ensure you have enough fabric for finishing. To stitch the entire design, center the design on the fabric and begin stitching. Determine the center of the design by locating the horizontal and vertical arrows on the chart. With your finger, trace along the grid to the point where the two centers meet. Compare a symbol at the center of the chart to the key and choose which floss color to stitch first. To find the center of the fabric, fold it into quarters and finger-crease.

▲

Stitch Count = 102 × 124

DESIGN SIZE

- 11-ct. = 9¼" × 11¼" (23.5cm × 28.6cm)
- 14-ct. = 7¼" × 8⅞" (18.4cm × 22.5cm)
- 16-ct. = 6⅜" × 7¾" (16.2cm × 19.7cm)

☐ Gray area indicates last row of previous section of design.

CROSS STITCH

ANCHOR		DMC	COLOR
5975	C	356	Light Medium Terra Cotta
8581	F	646	Dark Beaver Gray
900	H	648	Light Beaver Gray
303	L	742	Light Tangerine
882	P	758	Very Light Terra Cotta
307	T	783	Medium Topaz
1041	S	844	Ultra Dark Beaver Brown
4146	I	950	Light Desert Sand

BACKSTITCH

ANCHOR		DMC	COLOR
1041	—	844	Ultra Dark Beaver Brown

(use 1 strand for pencils and 2 strands for all other backstitches)

17

General Instructions

Getting Started

Cut the floss into 15" lengths and separate all six strands. Recombine the appropriate number of strands and thread them into a blunt-tip needle.

Unless otherwise indicated, cross stitches, three-quarter cross stitches, half cross stitches, and quarter cross stitches are worked with two strands of floss, and backstitches and French knots with one strand. For lettering that consists of backstitches only, use two strands of floss if you prefer thicker lettering. Work stitches over one thread if stitching on aida and over two threads if stitching on linen or evenweave.

To Secure Thread at the Beginning

The most common way to secure the beginning tail of the thread is to hold it on the wrong side of the fabric under the first four or five stitches.

To Secure Thread at the End

To finish, slip the threaded needle under previously stitched threads on the wrong side of the fabric for four or five stitches, weaving the thread back and forth a few times. Clip the thread.

Personalizing Designs

You can use the alphabets to stitch just a name, monogram, or date, or you can incorporate the letters into part of another stitched design.

To personalize a piece of fabric or a larger design, begin by counting the stitchable area you have to work with (stitches wide by stitches high). Mark this area on a piece of graph paper. Find the center of the stitchable area and the center of the name or monogram—this will determine if a letter or a space will be at the center.

Begin charting the name or monogram onto the graph paper, centering the middle letter or space and working outward. Use a pencil for this, as you may need to adjust the spacing so as to best utilize the area. In most cases, one or two empty rows between letters will work best, but some thin letters (I, L, T, etc.) may look better with more empty rows around them. Be consistent, and make sure the name or monogram looks even and balanced.

Match up the center of the fabric to the center of your graphed letters. Begin stitching at the center and work out to be sure the lettering is centered correctly on the fabric.

Cross Stitch

Make one cross stitch for each symbol on the chart. For horizontal rows, stitch the first diagonal of each stitch in the row. Work back

across the row, completing each stitch. On most linen and evenweave fabrics, work the stitches over two threads as shown in the diagram. For aida cloth, each stitch fills one square. You also can work cross stitches in the reverse direction. Remember to embroider the stitches uniformly—that is, always work the top half of each stitch in the same direction.

Quarter and Three-Quarter Cross Stitches

To obtain rounded shapes in a design, use quarter and three-quarter cross stitches. On linen and evenweave fabrics, a quarter

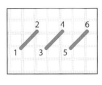

stitch will extend from the corner to the center intersection of the threads. To make quarter cross stitches on aida cloth, estimate the center of the square. Three-quarter cross stitches combine a quarter cross stitch with a half cross stitch. Both stitches may slant in any direction.

Half Cross Stitches

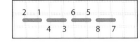

A half cross stitch is a single diagonal or half a cross stitch. They are indicated on the chart by a diagonal colored symbol.

Backstitches

Working from right to left, bring the needle up from the back side of the fabric, one stitch length from your starting point. Begin the next stitch by inserting the needle at your starting point and back up two stitch lengths away. Continue, keeping all the stitches the same length.

French Knot

Bring the threaded needle through the fabric and wrap the floss around the needle as shown. Tighten the twists and return the needle through the fabric in the same place. The floss will slide through the wrapped thread to make the knot.

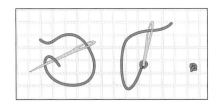

Straight Stitches

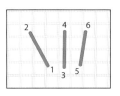

Bring the needle up from the back side of the fabric, then bring the needle down through the fabric in the desired spot to make a stitch of the desired length.

Project Ideas

• Stitch the initials of your favorite friend to create a monogrammed pin she will cherish.
• Create personalized dinner napkins by stitching your family's initials on a set of napkins.
• Accent a present with a personalized gift tag.
• Use the alphabets to create your own warm sentiment to send to family and friends. Chart a saying on graph paper, such as "Best Wishes," "Thank You," or "Get Well." Then stitch the saying on fabric and insert the piece into a greeting card with a photo opening. (Before charting your saying, be sure the stitched piece will fit in the photo opening.)
• Personalize a Christmas stocking for everyone in your family.
• Add a personal touch to a child's room by stitching their name and displaying it in their room.
• Don't limit yourself to cotton embroidery floss and aida or evenweave—try different fibers and fabrics, such as tapestry wool, metallic braid, plastic canvas, perforated paper, or needlepoint canvas. "Sam" (pictured above) was stitched on 5-mesh needlepoint canvas using needlepoint cross stitch and two undivided strands of tapestry wool.

Produced by Herrschners, Inc., for distribution exclusively by Leisure Arts, Inc., 5701 Ranch Drive, Little Rock, Arkansas 72223-9633, leisurearts.com.

We have made every effort to ensure that these instructions are accurate and complete.
We cannot, however, be responsible for human error, typographical mistakes, or variations in individual work.